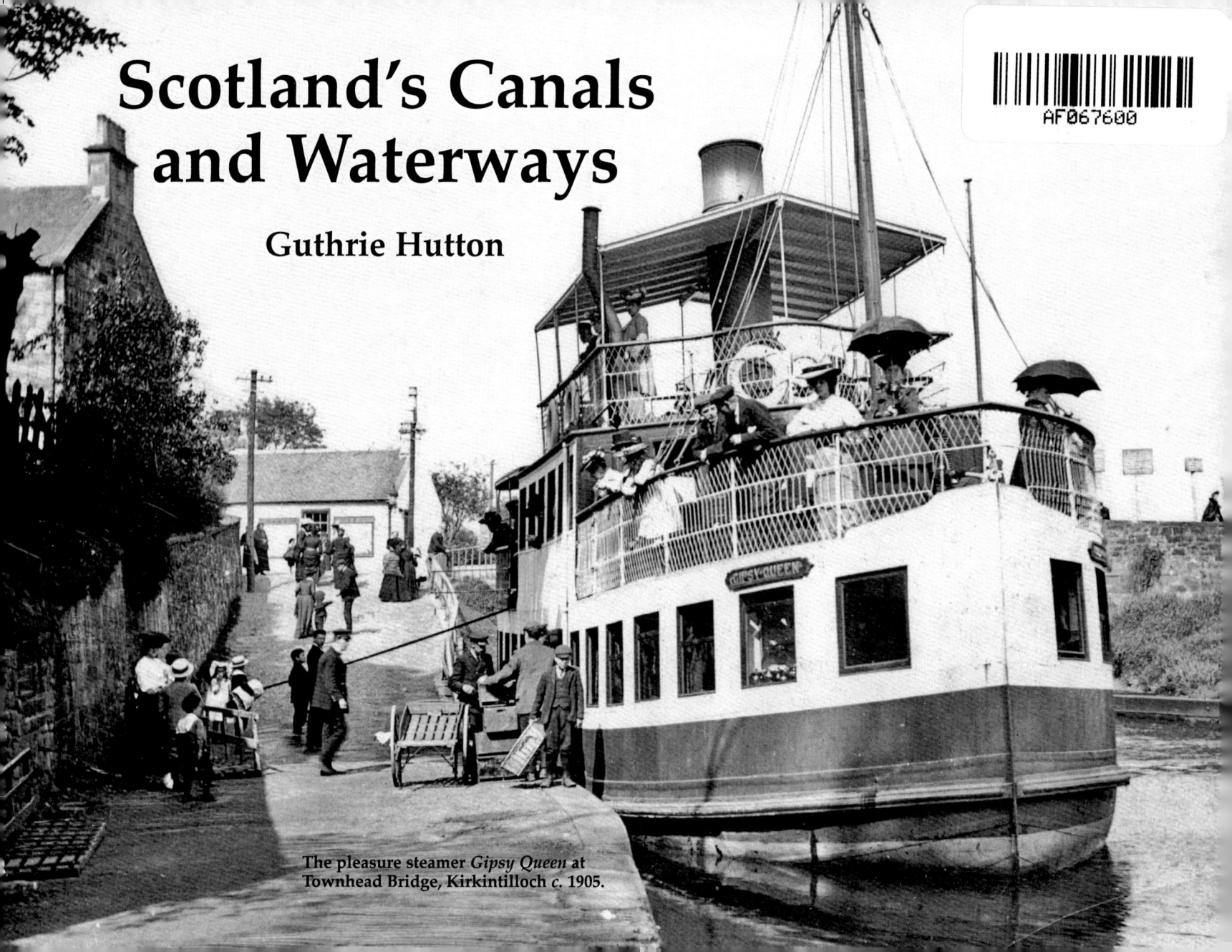

Scotland's Canals and Waterways

Guthrie Hutton

The pleasure steamer *Gipsy Queen* at Townhead Bridge, Kirkintilloch *c.* 1905.

© Guthrie Hutton, 2022
First published in the United Kingdom, 2022,
by Stenlake Publishing Ltd.
www.stenlake.co.uk
ISBN 978-1-84033-934-5

The publishers regret that they cannot supply copies of any pictures featured in this book.

Printed by
Blissetts, Unit E1-E8 Shield Drive,
West Cross Ind Pk, Brentford, TW8 9EX

Silhouettes and sunlight on the Glasgow, Paisley & Ardrossan Canal.

Further Reading

The following were the principal books and websites used by the author during his research. None are available from Stenlake Publishing; please contact your local bookshop, reference library or search for them on the internet.

Cameron, A. D., *The Caledonian Canal*, 1994.
Cameron, A. D., *Getting to Know.... The Crinan Canal*, 1978.
Clark, Sylvia, (Old Paisley Society) *The Paisley Canal (and etc.)*, 1985.
Clew, Kenneth R., (Dingwall Museum Trust), *The Dingwall Canal*, 1988.
Haynes, Nick, *Scotland's Canals*, 2015.
Lindsay, Jean, *The Canals of Scotland*, 1968.
Massey, Alison, *The Edinburgh and Glasgow Union Canal*, 1983.

Articles from *Waterways World* magazine.
Moss, Patrick, *The Aberdeenshire Canal*, August 1988.
Jayes, John, *Dingwall Canal*, March 1998.

Also by Guthrie Hutton, and published by Stenlake Publishing.
A Forth and Clyde Canalbum, 1991.
Forth and Clyde, The Comeback Canal, 1998.
The Old Forth & Clyde Canal, 2015.
Caledonian – The Monster Canal, 1992 (reprint 2009).
The Caledonian Canal; Lochs, Locks and Pleasure Steamers, 1998.
Monkland; The Canal That Made Money, 1993.
The Monkland Canal; Coal, Iron and Cold Hard Cash, 2015.
The Union Canal; A Capital Asset, 1993.
The Old Union Canal, 2017.
The Crinan Canal; Puffers and Paddle Steamers, 1994.
The Crinan Canal; The Shipping Short Cut, 2003.
Puffers, 2007.
Puffers and Places, 2018.
Scotland's Millennium Canals, 2002.

Acknowledgements

Canals have been a big part of my life, I have sailed on them, walked beside them, found solace in their tranquillity and been thrilled by their engineering magnificence. I have enjoyed many friendships with fellow enthusiasts and thank them all for enriching this story.

Introduction

Scotland didn't have many canals, but those that were made were magnificent and wonderfully varied in character. Through the central lowlands, the Great Glen and in Mid Argyll it was almost as if Mother Nature had laid out natural routes, expecting them to be canalised. The country was also rich in natural waterways like rivers and great estuaries, but inland this was not easy territory. Two canals, the Monkland and Union, were developed to transport coal and, once made, the former became a major factor in the growth of the iron industry. Both were in effect branches of the Forth & Clyde Canal, the country's first major waterway and a triumph of 18th century engineering. As a sea-to-sea canal connecting the coasts on either side of the country, it was made to stimulate trade and industry, as were the other sea-to-sea canals the Crinan and the mighty Caledonian – a wonder of its age. A desire to engage in trade was also behind development of the Glasgow, Paisley and Ardrossan Canal and many improvements to river navigations.

Some canals were successful, others less so, but time caught up with them all. Even the great Caledonian Canal had not been completed long before ships became too big for it. With the growth of railways the lowland canals rapidly declined and some disappeared, their routes used as track beds by railway companies. Against the odds most of the country's canals remained largely intact up to the mid 20th century, but then faced major challenges. The Crinan and Caledonian Canals were still operational, but age and lack of investment had taken their toll and by the end of the century both required major remedial work to make them fit for the future. In the lowlands, canals were seen as old, done, dirty and dangerous, resulting in the Monkland being largely destroyed, although a couple of short sections remained. The Forth & Clyde and Union Canals were closed in the 1960s and almost ruined, but within a decade enthusiasts had begun to agitate for their reinstatement. The campaign grew, culminating in navigation being restored through the lottery-funded Millennium Link project. Commenced in 1999, it was completed in 2002 with the unveiling, by the Queen, of the Falkirk Wheel boat lift. A country that had once taken a negative view of canals was now graced by one of the world's most recognisable canal structures which, added to a list of earlier treasures, is a remarkable transformation.

The paddle steamer *Gondolier* in the locks at Fort Augustus.

In June 1768 Sir Laurence Dundas of Kerse dug the first spadeful of earth to start cutting the Forth & Clyde Canal. The site chosen for the eastern sea lock was beside the tidal estuary of the River Carron, about a mile from its confluence with the Forth. At this point a tributary, the Grange Burn, flowed into the Carron and the village that grew up around the developing sea lock became known as Grangemouth. As the canal progressed, trade increased and the early terminal basins were soon augmented with new basins and a vast dock complex all linked to the canal. Sir Laurence had not just inaugurated the canal, but a big and important port as well. Heading away from the Carron the canal builders cut a broad channel, seen in this picture of a cruiser going west in the days just before closure, on 1st January 1963. On the left is a floating footbridge across the entrance to the large timber basins, while on the right is the bow of a ship being built beside the River Carron by the Grangemouth Dockyard Company. It was all ships, boats and water in Grangemouth's port area.

West from Grangemouth the ground rose only gently, but the navvies had some hard miles to cover at Falkirk where a string of locks was built to take the canal up from Bainsford to Camelon. The completed canal transformed the transportation of heavy materials, which helped to attract one industry in particular to Falkirk's canal banks: iron. Only a few years before work on the canal began, the great Carron Iron Works was started up on a site just across the river from Bainsford. From there the industry spread, with a number of foundries being set up, including that of the Falkirk Iron Company on a site adjacent to the Bainsford canal bridge. Driven on by its industry, Falkirk grew into a busy town, but one that became frustrated by delays to road transport caused by the wooden bascule canal bridges at Bainsford and Camelon. These early bridges were superseded in 1905 when the town council introduced a circular tram route with steel swing bridges at both locations. The Bainsford Bridge, and a conveniently posed tram, is seen here in a contemporary picture.

Bonnybridge, to the west of Falkirk, was a centre for the iron castings industry, with a number of foundries operating in the vicinity of the canal. There was Smith & Wellstood's Columbian Stove Works, which made kitchen ranges and stoves of all shapes and sizes. The popular 'Courtier' stove was made at the Bonnymuir Foundry of Mitchell, Russell & Co. Ltd, and similar appliances were made at Lane & Girvan's Caledonia Stove and Iron Works. As a canal with clear air draught (i.e. no height restrictions for vessels) the Forth & Clyde had a limited number of crossing points with opening bridges. It also had underpasses, one of which was at Bonnybridge. Known as the Bonnybridge Pend, it doubled as a culvert for a small burn. Water flowed through the pend on the paved roadway and, so that pedestrians would not get wet feet, there was a raised footpath. It was superseded by a wooden bascule bridge erected in close proximity to the Smith & Wellstood works in 1900 and that was replaced in 1936 by a steel swing bridge.

The summit reach of the canal stretches for sixteen miles from Lock 20 at Wyndford through to Glasgow. Creating the most easterly part of the summit across the Dullatur Bog proved to be a nightmare for the engineers and navvies. A liquid mess of moss and slime kept filling up the excavation and the only way to stabilise the work was to build embankments of earth and stones along both sides of the proposed channel and then dig it out and flood it. The large Townhead Reservoir was created to the east of Kilsyth and from there water was fed into the canal at the western end of the bog area. The countryside here is attractive and in 1895 an entrepreneur, James Aitken, began to use this location, Craigmarloch, as a destination for a fleet of pleasure steamers. The first was *Fairy Queen*, followed by another *Fairy Queen*, *May Queen* and lastly the largest vessel to ever sail the canal, *Gipsy Queen*. She is seen here at Craigmarloch where Aitken also built a tearoom and other recreational facilities.

To the west of Craigmarloch the canal follows the base of Croy Hill to Auchinstarry and then hugs the contours of neighbouring Bar Hill – two locations where remaining fragments of the Roman Antonine Wall are visible. The wall had been built about AD142 along a similar route to the canal and in places the canal builders casually wrecked surviving evidence. Twechar, at the base of Bar Hill, was a mining village supported by a large colliery with pits on both sides of the canal. The railway linking the complex crossed the canal on a swing bridge, that was built on condition that the mining company continued to ship coal by canal. There was also an original double-leaf opening road bridge, which limited the weight of vehicles that could cross it. The National Coal Board, which took over the nationalised coal industry in 1947, pressed for it to be replaced and got their way when the lifting bridge seen here was built in 1960, just in time for the closure of the canal in 1962/63, and the colliery in 1964.

Kirkintilloch sits halfway along the canal's summit pound. It was also a place of industry with large ironworks including the Lion Foundry where the once familiar red telephone boxes were made before being superseded by modern technology. The town was also steeped in canal-related activities. This was the 'Queen' pleasure steamers' home port. The early Monkland and Kirkintilloch Railway conveyed coal to the canal for onward transportation, so much humble cargo carrying was likewise based here. That in turn led to a boat-building industry situated at the railway basin and on a narrow piece of land adjacent to the Townhead Bridge that carried the main road through the town. As barges got bigger and fitted with steam engines they evolved into vessels, much loved in the folklore of West Central Scotland: puffers. One such boat, the *Briton*, is seen here going down the slips at the Townhead yard in 1893. The side-on launch always sent a huge wave across the canal, but on this occasion the photographer fired the shutter a split second too soon.

When construction work reached the edge of Glasgow, the canal company's finances were overstretched and so, instead of completing the sea-to-sea link, they turned toward the city on the summit level to make what was known as the Glasgow Branch. It was opened to a terminal basin at Hamilton Hill in 1777 allowing trade to develop between the east coast and the city, bringing in much-needed revenue. The volume of activity was such that Hamilton Hill soon proved to be inadequate and to provide extra capacity the canal was extended across Possil Road to Hundred Acre Hill where extensive new basins known as Port Dundas were created. Streets were laid out allowing houses, warehouses and factories to be erected. Industry moved in, but being to the north of the city, where prevailing winds would take away unpleasant emissions, the area attracted businesses like the chemical works in Crawford Street seen in this mid 19th century engraving looking across to Mid Wharf. Port Dundas wasn't pretty, but it drove the canal's economy.

Work to continue making the canal down to the Clyde began in 1785, with funding assistance coming from the sale of estates forfeited after the Jacobite uprising of 1745/46. The point where the Glasgow Branch and main line joined became known as Stockingfield Junction. From there a short section of canal went west to a flight of five locks. With a small boatyard and dry dock incorporated in the construction they became a major feature and sparked the development of a new village that became known as Maryhill, named after the heiress of the local Gairbraid Estate. At the foot of the locks the engineers and navvies faced their biggest construction challenge, bridging the valley of the River Kelvin. It wasn't the first aqueduct to be built on the canal; there had been others, notably the Luggie Aqueduct at Kirkintilloch, but it was by a long way the biggest. The all masonry structure was so big and impressive that people wrote odes in its honour and engraved illustrations like the one shown here.

The engineer who planned the canal was John Smeaton, but by the time that work started on the western section he had retired and been replaced by Robert Whitworth. He made some changes to Smeaton's plan, including bypassing Dalmuir as the proposed location for the sea-lock on the Clyde and continuing west to Bowling. On the way the canal crossed routes to river ferries and that meant installing opening bridges like the one shown here on Ferry Road, Old Kilpatrick leading to the Erskine Ferry. Known as bascule bridges – bascule is a French word meaning seesaw – they served the canal well until increasing road traffic meant that some were replaced by larger lifting (bascule) or swing bridges, one of which was installed at Ferry Road in 1934. Old Kilpatrick was also the site of the western fort and terminal of the Antonine Wall and the canal cut through some Roman remains. There was another bascule bridge to the west of the village at Ferrydyke, a name that may reflect proximity to the wall and an associated river crossing.

The canal was officially opened in 1790 when a hogshead of water taken from the Forth was emptied into the Clyde at Bowling to symbolise the union of the eastern and western seas. The sea lock was at one end of the terminal basin and another lock spanned by an opening bridge was at the other. Years later when the canal was owned by the Caledonian Railway Company these arrangements were altered. A new outer harbour was made and another sea lock, sheltered by the harbour, was built. The upper lock was moved east and a large new high-sided basin built, leaving the original lock chamber, still spanned by the bascule bridge as a narrow channel between the basins. A massive railway swing bridge crossed the channel at a high level and another railway swing bridge for goods traffic to the outer harbour was installed. Its purpose was industrial, but by 1960 when the canal's closure loomed, the basin was largely the domain of leisure craft as this picture shows. Even after closure the basins remained open for such boats, as a tiny rump of working canal.

The most industrial canal in Scotland and consequently the most financially successful was the Monkland Canal. Work on it began in 1770 with James Watt as engineer, before he achieved fame developing steam power. After three distinct construction phases, the canal was completed between Calderbank and Port Dundas by 1793, finally achieving its objective of getting coal from the Monklands into Glasgow in sufficient volume to break the monopolistic cartel of the city's coal masters. The other big industry was iron, which came to dominate the town of Coatbridge. It grew with astonishing speed following the discovery locally of blackband ironstone and the development of the hot blast smelting process. Huge blast furnace plants were set up alongside the canal or its many branches at Calder, Gartsherrie, Dundyvan, Langloan and the works seen in this picture from about 1910, Summerlee. Of these the largest and longest lasting was Gartsherrie, but Summerlee has become better known as the site of a splendid industrial museum.

Coatbridge was a crossroads in more ways than one. Roads, railways and the canal all met at the one central location resulting in a remarkable assemblage of bridges as the various forms of transport found different routes and levels through the junction. As well as the great iron works, there were numerous canalside foundries that turned the pig iron from the blast furnaces into an array of iron products. Many of these plants were cooled by water from the canal, which when returned made it steam like the River Styx. Along with the fire, smoke, dirt and noise it contributed to a description of the town as 'hell with the lid off'. At Sheepford, near Coatdyke, a pair of locks was built to allow the canal to be extended eastwards. It gave access to new coal mines and at Faskine, close to the terminal at Calderbank, there was an ironworks where Scotland's first iron boat, the *Vulcan*, was built. A replica was made for the Glasgow Garden Festival in 1988 and subsequently taken to Summerlee as an exhibit.

Ominously for the canal, the Monklands was not just where the coal and iron industries expanded so quickly, it was also the cradle of Scottish railways. Pioneering lines spread out from the Coatbridge area toward Glasgow, Kirkintilloch and other parts of Lanarkshire although the volume of trade was so great it kept the canal busy through much of the 19th century. When decline set in though, it was inexorable. The canal was abandoned in 1950 and significant lengths were filled in with the water piped to maintain the flow through to the Forth & Clyde Canal. Much of the infilling in Coatbridge was done to the point west of the town centre seen in this picture, with the suburb of Blairhill on one side and West End Park on the other. Originally part of Drumpellier Estate the parkland became so well used by local people that the estate owner recognised reality and gifted it to the town. Lying to the west of the town, Drumpellier Estate has since become a country park incorporating a small but pleasing remaining section of canal.

James Watt's original canal was extended in the 1780s from its western end outside Glasgow to the top of the slope at Blackhill and from the foot of the hill to the city's Castle Street, with coal wagons linking the two sections. Following an agreement with the Forth & Clyde Canal Company in 1790, the wagons were replaced with locks and the lower canal extended west to Port Dundas. The eastward extension of the main canal from Coatbridge was used as a feeder, taking water from the North Calder to the Forth and Clyde Canal. A major system had been created, but the Blackhill Locks were unable to cope with the growing coal and iron traffic and a second lock flight was built alongside the first. That wasn't enough and in 1850 an inclined plane with iron caissons mounted on wheeled cradles and running on rails was installed. The caissons contained enough water to support an empty boat and were hauled up the hill by a stationary steam engine that operated for about 30 years until trade declined and it became uneconomic. Blackhill is seen here about 1910.

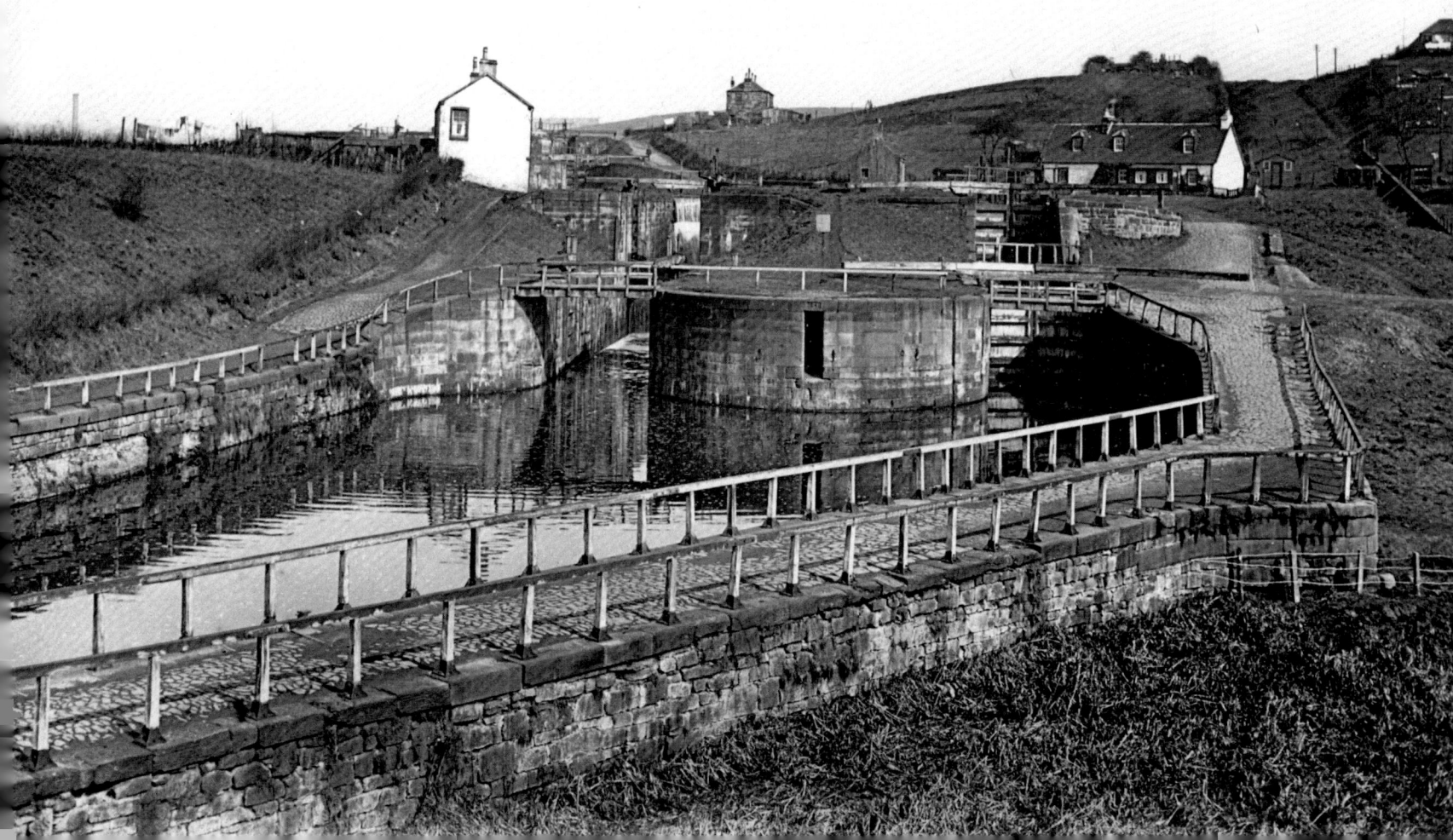

Although late 18th century efforts to deepen the Clyde were largely successful, it remained a difficult river to navigate in a sailing vessel. That prompted the 12th Earl of Eglinton to believe he could create a major port on the coast of his Ayrshire estate linked to Glasgow by canal. He formed a committee and engaged engineers to survey the route. Thomas Telford modified their initial report and the proposed canal received parliamentary assent in 1806. The route ran between Ardrossan Bay and Tradeston in Glasgow with branches to coal workings at Hurlet and Cambuslang. Work started in the east because that would link the population centres of Johnstone and Paisley with Glasgow and thus generate income to finance the more difficult section over higher ground to the coast, including the construction of locks west of Johnstone and at Ardrossan. The lock-free eastern section was eleven miles long and although there were many bends, the level track made for easy boat movements. It opened between Johnstone and Paisley in October 1810 and to Port Eglinton, as the Glasgow basin was known, a year later.

In his plans, Telford recognised the need to attract trade and selected a route close to existing coal workings and other industries. The cotton mills of Johnstone and Paisley were humming and with other industries starting up, the canal was in a good place to serve potential customers. Despite that, revenues from the first ten years of operations were insufficient to meet the costs of constructing the western section of canal and the proposed branches. Attempts to raise money through private loans or grants from public funds also failed to provide the necessary finance and so the plans were abandoned in 1820, but not the route. Another parliamentary act of 1827 authorised the company to construct a railway and although limited funds meant that only the section between Kilwinning and Ardrossan was made, it did provide a transport route for the Eglinton collieries. For a canal company to build a railway might seem like a turkey voting for Christmas, but it was a recognition that the next transport revolution was literally coming down the tracks.

Routes to and from the Ayrshire coast, and between Paisley and Glasgow, inevitably attracted railway companies and so, despite owning its own tracks the canal company had to ward off proposals from railway promoters irked to discover that the canal already occupied the best ground. It proved to be a losing battle and in 1869 the Glasgow & South Western Railway Company acquired the canal. They agreed to keep it operational, but after a dozen years used the route to build a railway. It incorporated some canal structures, most notably the Blackhall Aqueduct over the River Cart and by straightening bends left a few cut-off meanders. The most obvious clues to the canal's former existence are in the names of Paisley Canal Station, Canal Street in Paisley and Port Eglinton. One small stretch of canal that lingered longer than most was beside the Ferguslie thread mills which is seen here in a picture that, like the others shown here, was taken at the time of closure in 1882. A canal culvert beside the mill was where Paisley poet Robert Tannahill took his own life in May 1810. The canal had not yet opened, but there would be more tragedy when it did.

On 10th November 1810, only a few days after the canal's opening, a boat from Johnstone arrived at Paisley. It was a holiday and enthusiastic crowds rushed to get on board, with many clambering onto the cabin roof. Aware of the danger the anxious boatmen pushed off from the bank, but no longer supported by the jetty, the boat capsized tipping dozens of mainly young people into the water. Eighty-four drowned in the worst disaster on a Scottish canal. It was a dreadful start, but in later years passenger boat services on the canal were to make the news for good reasons. In an effort to compete with coaches on the lucrative route between Paisley and Glasgow the canal company conducted experiments to find a hull shape that would slip through the water at speed. The successful design was a sleek iron boat 70 feet long, with a beam of six feet and drawing about eighteen inches fully loaded with 90 people. Hauled by two fleet-footed post horses it could complete the journey in 45 minutes and established a pattern of fast boat operations that was copied by other British canal operators. The picture shows the last passenger boat excursion.

Set in glorious scenery, the Crinan Canal runs for nine miles across Knapdale at the north end of the Kintyre peninsula from Ardrishaig in the east to Loch Crinan. Planned as an alternative to the long and potentially perilous passage around the Mull of Kintyre, it was begun in 1794 by a private company led by the Duke of Argyll. It opened in 1801, but poorly made, it closed a couple of times and was in a bad way when the great Thomas Telford conducted a survey. He could have recommended closure, but instead proposed improvements that when made by 1817 secured the canal's future. Thirty years later Queen Victoria and Prince Albert sailed along the canal on a horse-drawn barge, a trip that inspired steamer operators David Hutcheson & Co., followed by David MacBrayne, to create the 'Royal Route', a succession of steamers operating between the Clyde and Inverness. *Linnet*, seen here about 1880 at Ardrishaig, was built in 1866 to form a link in that chain. She was sold in 1929 when the 'Royal Route' had lost its appeal.g.

One type of vessel that became popularly associated with the canal was the puffer, and one of those boats, the *Pibroch*, passed through the canal so often she was a familiar sight. She is seen here in 1950 sitting above Lock 4 at Ardrishaig with the canal stretching ahead of her to the west. Puffers could carry all sorts of cargoes from coal and bricks to slates and sand, and everything in between to many destinations, but *Pibroch* was different. She operated on a set route and was confined to a discreet range of cargoes for her owners the White Horse Distillery on Islay – supplies in and barrels of whisky out. Weighing 96 tons, she was built at Bowling by Scott and Sons and launched in 1923 and unlike other well-worn puffers was always a smart looking boat. She was sold in 1957 renamed *Texa* and then *Cumbrae Lass* before going to the breaker's yard at Dalmuir in 1967. Her replacement on distillery duties was a diesel coaster also built by Scotts and also named *Pibroch*.

Ardrishaig sits at the mouth of Loch Gilp, a short inlet leading off Loch Fyne. It is too shallow, even at high tide, for vessels of any size to reach Lochgilphead, but the canal was sufficiently close, and it served the town. There was a bridge here that connected paths to and from Ardrishaig on either side of the canal and one of the improvements recommended by Thomas Telford was to erect a wharf beside the bridge. It had the added bonus for the bridge keeper of having to look after the boats and their cargoes and one of those keepers, William Miller, took to this task with such dedication, and did it for so long, that the bridge became known as 'Miller's Bridge' although the official name is Oakfield Bridge. The wharf became Lochgilphead's coal depot with cargoes delivered by puffers and before that by 'gabbarts', a word used to describe a variety of sailing craft engaged in the coastal trade before steam-power took over. The splendid boat seen here at the wharf could have been one such vessel.

In common with the Forth & Clyde, the Crinan was a sea-to-sea canal designed for the use of vessels with masts, consequently only seven bridges were built and they all had to open. To begin with these appear to have been made of wood, but were replaced as part of Thomas Telford's improvements and have subsequently been upgraded to meet the challenges imposed by bigger and heavier road vehicles. This swing bridge across the chamber of Lock 5 at Cairnbaan was installed in the late 19th century and superseded in the 1930s by a larger swing bridge mounted on new abutments just above the lock. There are four locks with intermediate pounds at Cairnbaan and although the locks were always set for the arrival of the *Linnet* it still took time for her to negotiate them. Consequently, passengers often took the opportunity to get off and walk, and while ashore, sample the delights of the inn beside Lock 5, the little store beside Lock 8 or produce stalls set up by local people.

The summit level of the canal, to the west of the Cairnbaan locks, is seen here with the puffer *Glencloy* heading east. Built in 1930 for the Arran-based company, G. & G. Hamilton she often used the canal, on this occasion in 1955 shortly before being converted to diesel when her tall funnel was replaced with a stubby one. The summit pound is short, under a mile in length, but incorporated in it at the western end is the small Loch a'Bharain, which acts as a reservoir so that the summit holds sufficient water for the locks at either end to use. Reservoirs were also created in the hills to the south, to supply the canal. Water was a perennial problem on the Crinan; it leaked and required frequent repair. With limited sources of water it could struggle to remain viable in a dry spell, but conversely situated in an area of high rainfall, there were times when there was too much water and a unique mechanism, known as the water waster, released water into Loch Gilp to ensure that the reach between Ardrishaig and Cairnbaan didn't overtop and cause a flood.

Puffers, gabbarts, fishing boats and the *Linnet* were all common sights on the canal, but, as some of those vessels faded into history, pleasure boats began to appear in ever increasing numbers. Here a yacht is seen in August 1921 working through one of the five Dunardry Locks. These are situated at the western end of the summit reach and for a boat like this one, going west, the views from here are superb, holding out the prospect of idyllic sailing amongst glorious scenery. She is a handsome boat and, given that her owners could also afford a camera, it's fair to assume that they were well off. They were well dressed too, wearing ties and the kind of clothing that no modern sailor would choose. Since those days yachting has become a more popular activity and, with people regarding the west coast of Scotland as being amongst the finest sailing waters in the world, the canal has become so busy that a yacht haven equipped with pontoons was established at Bellanoch, between Dunardry and Crinan.

Bellanoch Bridge (front cover) was one of the more significant canal crossings. Resting on abutments carved out of solid rock, it carries the road that runs south through Knapdale to Tayvallich and Castle Sween, and north over the River Add, across the Moine Mhor (the Great Moss) and past the ancient fortress of Dunadd to Kilmartin. It is a landscape occupied since prehistoric times, replete with archaeological interest. The small community of Bellanoch is more recent having grown up alongside both the canal bridge and, to the west, beside the wide lagoon, where the yacht haven was later developed. The lagoon was formed when the canal builders constructed an embankment across the mouth of Bellanoch Bay allowing the water to fill in behind it. It saved a lot of digging, but the bank was not well made and had a history of leaking. A few buildings including this row of thatched cottages stood beside the lagoon, presenting the well-to-do yacht owners and Royal Route travellers with a contrast to their own urban life styles.

West of Bellanoch, the canal hugged the shoreline and in places was cut through solid rock to reach Crinan. A lock, also hacked out of rock and topped with masonry, sits above the terminal basin, which over the years has been crowded with puffers, fishing boats and yachts. Buildings cluster around it, the largest being the hotel, which was originally owned by the canal company, but since 1900 has been run by private operators and enlarged and extended a number of times. The sea lock was made bigger than the inland locks so that boats could come in from the open sea and use the basin as a harbour. It was superseded in the 1930s by a new lock positioned alongside the original, which was left in place as an extension to the terminal basin. It is seen here on the right occupied by an Oban registered fishing boat, while the distinctive little hexagonal lighthouse stands guard and a yacht heads out of the new sea lock into Loch Crinan and a west coast sailing adventure.

The Caledonian is the longest, widest and deepest canal in Scotland; in the west it's even got the country's highest mountain, Ben Nevis, as a backdrop, so big that not all of it could fit into this picture of the railway swing bridge at Banavie. The sea lock is a mile to the west at Corpach, where the large terminal basin was excavated out of solid rock by navvies wielding hand tools. From there a pair of locks lifts the canal to the level crossed by the railway bridge. The line is an extension of the West Highland Railway, which had been opened between Glasgow and Fort William in 1894. It was always the railway promoters' ambition to take it to a point on the west coast where a fishing industry could be developed, but it took some time to select Mallaig as the most suitable site. Construction of the extension started at Corpach in 1897 and the line, famous for its reinforced concrete viaducts, was opened in April 1901. A swing bridge carrying the road to Mallaig over the canal sits alongside the railway bridge, making for a dramatic spectacle when they both swing aside to allow a boat to sail through.

The other dramatic sight at Banavie is the flight of eight locks popularly known as Neptune's Staircase. The poet Robert Southey, a friend of Thomas Telford, the engineer who designed the canal, described the lock flight as the 'greatest work of art in Britain'. It may not be quite that, but it is certainly impressive and is seen here in a view from the 1930s that looks down toward Loch Linnhe and Loch Eil. Some boats are working through the locks and a team of men use poles to rotate a capstan, which wound in a chain connected to the lock gate to either open or close it. This laborious system has since been replaced by hydraulic mechanisms. Staircase locks like those at Banavie, and other flights on the Caledonian Canal, are built as a single entity with each lock having gates in common with the neighbouring locks. They were cheaper to build, but formed operational bottlenecks because a large boat had to go through the whole flight before another could pass in the opposite direction.

Passenger steamers conveyed tourists up and down the canal as part of the 'Royal Route' between Glasgow and Inverness, but it would have taken too long to use the Banavie locks so instead they operated from a wharf above the top lock. For people coming from or going on to Crinan a coach service operated between Corpach and the steamer wharf at Banavie. Later a spur from the Mallaig railway was built up to the wharf. At the height of operations in the late 19th and early 20th centuries, two paddle steamers worked the route, *Gondolier* and *Gairlochy*. They set off in the morning from either Inverness or Banavie, one going north and other heading south, and they passed each other roughly halfway along the canal on Loch Oich. It was an arrangement that came to an abrupt halt on Christmas Eve 1919 when *Gairlochy* caught fire at Fort Augustus and was burnt to the waterline, a sad end for a fine ship. She is seen here between trips, moored up on the offside of the canal at Banavie.

A steamer trip along the canal was a scenic delight, but it could require a degree of fortitude as these pictures of well-clad passengers wrapped up and sheltering from the wind show. They were taken in 1899 on board the *Gondolier,* the steamer that became most closely associated with the canal sailings. Built on the Clyde in 1866 by J. & G. Thomson she was a handsome vessel although unusually for the time had a blunt bow and stern to make her fit the locks. Originally she sailed in concert with an older steamer, the *Glengarry* before being partnered by *Gairlochy* between 1895 and her fire in 1919. After that *Gondolier* carried on alone until she was withdrawn in 1939, at the outbreak of the Second World War. She was taken over by the Admiralty, stripped of her engines, saloon and paddle boxes, and towed to the Orkney Islands where she was scuttled as a block ship to protect the Scapa Flow naval anchorage after HMS *Royal Oak* had been sunk by submarine.

Work on the Caledonian Canal began in 1803. Designed by the great engineer Thomas Telford it runs along the length of the Great Glen as a series of man-made canals connecting Loch Lochy, Loch Oich and Loch Ness. It was opened in 1822 but not at the planned depth and was closed again between 1844 and 1847 for repairs and improvements. There are few populous places along the route, but one village grew and prospered from proximity to the canal, Fort Augustus. Here the flight of five locks provided steamer passengers with an opportunity to get off and patronise the shops on both sides of the canal while their boat made its slow progress up or down the locks. In later years, as car-borne tourism developed it became a popular place to stop, shop, eat and watch the passing boats. Throughout the canal's history a large proportion of those vessels have been fishing boats like those seen here heading west in 1905, one driven by sail the other by steam.

At the foot of the Fort Augustus locks is Loch Ness, the biggest of the three lochs linked together to form the canal. It's not just the largest in the Great Glen, it's the most voluminous body of fresh water in the British Isles (1.78 cubic miles), more than double that of Lough Neagh, bigger than all the lakes and reservoirs in England put together. It's like an inland sea, 24 miles long, up to a mile and half wide, deeper than the North Sea and with a surface area of 35 square miles. Ships and boats have always used its waters, as shown by this picture from 1912 of a small freighter alongside Invermoriston Pier, one of a number of piers that served loch-side communities. Paddle steamers from Inverness also operated a passenger and mail service to the piers, until superseded by motor vehicles and road improvements in the 1930s. The loch has long attracted tourists with the Falls of Foyers a big draw until diminished by the country's first hydroelectric plant, and Drumnadrochit has made an industry out of the loch's most famous inhabitant; the monster!

The canal engineers built a weir across the River Ness to fix the water level in the loch; it also created the small Loch Dochfour. North of the weir, Dochgarroch Lock regulates the water level in the canal, which carries on through to the Beauly Firth. On the edge of Inverness it passes the distinctive hill known as Tomnahurich, which was apparently the subject of a 17th century prediction by the prophet, the Brahan Seer who declared that one day fully rigged-ships would be seen sailing inland behind it. If true, he got that right as this photograph of a handsome steam yacht beside the hill shows. To the left is one of the canal's original cast iron bridges, made in two halves and mounted on opposite banks. These required the bridge keeper to swing open one side and then row across to open the other half, a time-consuming operation that was superseded at Tomnahurich in 1937 when Sir William Arrol & Company installed a new swing bridge, designed by engineers Crouch and Hogg.

At Inverness, the *Gondolier* and other steamers operated from a wharf above the four Muirtown Locks. They are seen here in a picture from the 1970s with an Oban registered fishing boat heading east down the flight, bucking the more usual trend of east coast boats going west. At the foot of the locks the boat would have passed through another road swing bridge, which like the one at Tomnahurich was replaced in the 1930s. It sits at one end of the huge Muirtown Basin that covers an area of twenty acres. The canal engineers believed it would provide a major harbour for the town, but after all that digging it never fulfilled their hopes. At the eastern end of the basin are the Clachnaharry Works Lock and the swing bridge for the railway line to Wick and Thurso. Beyond that the engineers built a huge embankment out across the soft muddy shore of the Beauly Firth to a point where it was deep enough to create the sea lock. It was a phenomenal achievement and it has stood the test of time.

Twenty-two miles north of Inverness, Dingwall was an important town, but despite close proximity to the Cromarty Firth, it did not have a harbour and struggled to conduct trade. The idea of erecting a pier was rejected, but more success attended a proposal to make a canal from the mouth of the River Conon, hugging the shoreline to meet the River Peffrey. It was to be a tidal inlet, just over a mile long with harbour facilities close to the town. Work began in September 1815 and Thomas Telford who had been peripherally involved declared it complete in December 1816, but suggested improvements which were implemented by the following March. Inadequate arrangements for earning revenue meant that the canal was poorly maintained and tended to silt up despite, or perhaps because a flow from the River Peffrey was directed along it. The railway arrived in the 1860s, bridged the canal and reduced its trade. It continued to decline and in the 1880s was effectively abandoned, but nature hadn't reclaimed it when this picture was taken in the early 20th century.

The Aberdeenshire Canal ran alongside the River Don between a terminal close to Aberdeen Harbour and the junction of the Don and Urie Rivers at Inverurie where the terminal basin was named Port Elphinstone. It was just over eighteen miles long and had seventeen locks, 60 feet long and nine feet wide, close to Aberdeen. It was opened in May 1805, but the locks proved to be poorly made and had to be rebuilt the following year. Initially it was not connected to Aberdeen Harbour, but a tidal lock was made in 1834 allowing cargoes to be directly transhipped in or out of canal barges without the need for double handling. Ten years later the writing appeared, if not on the wall then in the prospectus for the Great North of Scotland Railway between Aberdeen and Huntly. The first section of line between Huntly and Inverurie was begun in 1852 and two years later the railway company bought the canal with a view to laying tracks along its bed. Inverurie, once a canal port with mills and granaries, became a railway town. It is seen here from the air with Port Elphinstone in the foreground.

Down on the Solway Coast, people thought that the Annan, Nith, Dee and Fleet Valleys would be suitable for canal development, but other than some improvements to river navigations little else got beyond proposals. One early scheme that did get made involved cutting a one and a half mile channel known as Carlingwark Lane between Carlingwark Loch and the River Dee, with another cut made to bypass bends in the river and provide communication by water between Castle Douglas and New Galloway. Further west, the Water of Fleet was navigable between Gatehouse and the sea, but a major improvement for shipping was implemented in 1824. The local landowner brought men over from his Irish estates to straighten out river meanders and reclaim land covered at high tide. The work was overseen by the estate factor who, showing great engineering skill, had the channel cut to general dimensions and then let in the water to finish the job. Boats of up to 160 tons could use the waterway, which is seen here about 1900 at the harbour known as Port Macadam, with Gatehouse in the background.

Scotland didn't have an extensive network of inland waterways, but it did have the sea and by connecting one side of the country with the other the sea-to-sea canals extended coastal shipping routes. This meant that most communities of any size could trade with each other, and not just Scottish, but English, Irish and European ports too. Ships could reach far inland on river navigations like the Water of Fleet and especially on the larger estuaries. The Tay was navigable beyond Perth and in the town itself an inlet was cut along the line of what is now Canal Street. Boats could travel up the Forth to Stirling and when bridges were built at Alloa and Kincardine they had to have opening spans. The Clyde was channelled and deepened to permit large ships to navigate up to Glasgow and its tributary the Leven was navigable up to, and with a bit of effort into Loch Lomond. On the south bank the White Cart was made navigable up to Paisley Harbour, with fixtures like this impressive bascule bridge installed at Inchinnan by Sir William Arrol & Company and seen here on its opening day in March 1923.

It took a long time for a canal proposal to find favour in Edinburgh. A flurry of schemes rejected in the 1790s went into abeyance during the Napoleonic Wars, but a severe winter in 1812/13, coupled with very high coal prices concentrated minds. The earlier proposals were dusted off, but were still too costly and a compromise plan to cut a canal from the Fountainbridge area of the city to join the Forth & Clyde at Falkirk finally got under way in March 1818. The Edinburgh and Glasgow Union Canal, better known simply as the Union Canal, was the last major canal to be started in Scotland but, constructed more rapidly than earlier ones, was opened in 1822. It is seen here in a contemporary engraving looking toward Port Hopetoun, the terminal basin in Edinburgh. With the Semple Street bridge spanning the basin entrance, a dominant castle and distant silhouette of St Giles Cathedral, the drawing may seem contrived, but it is accurate. Later, as the coal trade developed, a basin known as Port Hamilton was made on the left, while on the right the canal heads west.

In 1922, 100 years after Port Hopetoun opened, it was closed along with Port Hamilton and the whole section of canal east of Fountainbridge. Lochrin Basin, seen here in a picture from 1919, became the new terminal. On parade beside the basin are army cadets associated with the North British Rubber Company whose large factory is on the left. It started out in 1855 as Norris & Company making rubber goods in the Castle Mills, a former silk mill, and changed the name to North British Rubber in 1857. The site was later taken over by the Fountain Brewery and in modern times the area has been transformed by offices and housing. In the centre of the picture, just visible through Auld Reekie's winter haze is a small opening bridge that was replaced by the large Leamington lifting bridge, moved from its original site at Fountainbridge after closure of the city basins. On the right, the hut with a lifebelt hanging at the apex of the gable was a boating station where people could hire a rowing boat and sail into the sunset, or just paddle around the basin.

The canals were a big improvement to transport between Edinburgh and Glasgow. There were roads of course; about three principal routes, but neither they nor the vehicles available at the time could carry heavy loads or the many people who now wanted to travel. Next came the Edinburgh & Glasgow Railway followed by piecemeal improvements to roads before the new A8 was made in the 1920s. It crossed the canal on a new bridge from where this picture was taken, looking toward Bridge 25, known as Miss Margaret's Bridge. The A8 by-passed most towns including Broxburn, which is seen in the background with the chimneys of the great Broxburn Oil Company's works prominent. Formed in 1877 out of a number of earlier concerns, the company grew to become one of the biggest in the West Lothian shale oil industry. Other such works were established beside the canal at Winchburgh and Philpstoun, but none made much use of the canal, which always struggled for want of industrial users. A legacy of large bings of spent shale remains.

Opened in 1842 and running beside the Union Canal for much of its length, the Edinburgh & Glasgow Railway could have spelled the end, but instead the railway company bought the canal in 1849, let it decline, but paradoxically saved it from oblivion. One place where the railway came very close to the canal was Linlithgow where the Manse Road basin was a centre of activity in the canal's early days. That had all but gone by the mid 20th century as this picture looking west from the deserted basin shows. Closure of the canal in 1965 was meant to be terminal, but ten years later a group of enthusiasts formed a society to campaign for reopening. They put boats on the water, opened a museum and tearoom, and generally filled the basin with activity. Full reopening of the canals as part of the Millennium Link project has attracted more visitors. Many come by train and for them it's a short walk up from the station, the railway and canal finally working to their mutual benefit.

Situated to the west of Linlithgow, the Avon Aqueduct is one of three large aqueducts that are the Union Canal's crowning glories. The Avon is the biggest, 85 feet high, 810 feet long and with twelve arches; it is also the second longest aqueduct in Britain. Designed by canal engineer Hugh Baird, whose plans were endorsed by Thomas Telford, these great structures were all built to a standard pattern. Internally buttressed hollow masonry piers were set apart by arches of 50 feet diameter. A trough made up of iron plates, bolted together and caulked to make the joints watertight, was laid across the top and encased in stone, giving the whole a uniform appearance, more elegant than the Forth & Clyde's all masonry Kelvin Aqueduct of just 35 years earlier. Of the other aqueducts, the Slateford over the Water of Leith is 65 feet high, 600 feet long and consists of eight arches, and the five-arched Almond Aqueduct west of Ratho is 76 feet high and 420 feet long.

The need to get coal into Edinburgh at an affordable price was the primary reason for building the Union Canal. One locality that responded enthusiastically to the capital's cry was Polmont and the Braes where many coal workings were developed. Those early pits or mines had been worked out long before James Nimmo and Company took a lease on Redding Colliery in 1894 and two years later sank a new No. 23 shaft between the canal and the railway. On 25th September 1923 the miners were stripping coal up to an underground fault when water from old workings burst into the pit. Some men managed to run ahead of the flood and escape, and 21 were brought up an old shaft, but 45 were missing. A huge rescue effort was mounted, involving divers from the naval base at Rosyth. Five men were found after nine days, but 40 had drowned in the worst flooding disaster in a Scottish pit. The colliery, seen here at the time of the accident, went back to work and was closed in 1958.

When William Forbes objected to plans for the canal to pass through the grounds of his grand Callendar House on the east side of Falkirk, he forced the engineers to cut a tunnel through the solid rock of Prospect Hill. Tunnelling was not new, miners had always done it, but this was huge, over 690 yards long, big enough for the passage of large boats and with a towing path for their horses. The men who dug it were mainly Irish labourers because according to contemporary accounts local men found the job a bit too hard. They worked from each end and from the bottom of two shafts sunk from the surface. It was slow going, because the rock was hard, but that meant it could stand unsupported with lining needed at only a few weak spots. It wasn't Scotland's only canal tunnel; there were two short ones on the Glasgow, Paisley and Ardrossan Canal and another on the Langloan Branch of the Monkland Canal, but it was by any measure the largest. This picture of a rower from 1905 looks through the tunnel from its eastern portal to the distant light at the end.